RAINBOW SCIENCE

Discover How Rainbows Are Made
with 23 Fun Experiments & Colorful Activities!

Artemis Roehrig

Illustrations by Sarah Walsh

Storey Publishing

HELLO, RAINBOW SCIENTIST!

Scientists look at rainbows to discover something new. The next scientist to make discoveries is YOU!

In this book, you will learn all about the science of rainbows and how to do colorful experiments. You'll learn how to find rainbows and make rainbows. You'll even be able to see rainbows anywhere with your rainbow glasses!

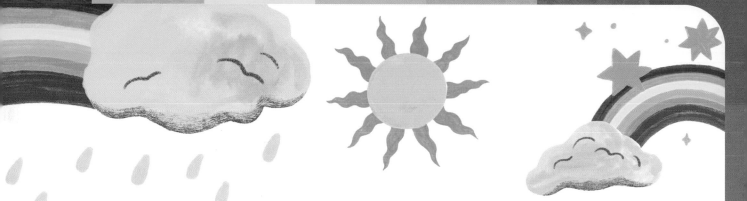

You can be a rainbow scientist! Do you wonder how rainbows are made or how your eyes see color? Read the **What's the Science?** pages, then try the experiments that follow.

Once you've tried them, see what happens if you do the experiments differently. Share your ideas with your friends, and together you can invent new experiments!

The study of rainbows is called **spectroscopy.**

Ready to find or make a rainbow? Turn the page!

How Are Rainbows Made?

When you see a rainbow in the sky, it may seem like magic. But there's real science in how rainbows are formed!

Rainbows are made when sunlight shines through raindrops. Sunlight contains all the colors of the rainbow.

On a rainy day with a little sun, the raindrops split the light. All the colors separate, and you see a rainbow.

How do raindrops split sunlight so you see the colors?

1.

The light **refracts** (or changes direction) as it travels through the front side of the raindrop. Each color of light bends at a different angle.

2.

The **refracted** light **reflects** off the back of the raindrop.

3.

The light **refracts** again as it travels through the front side of the raindrop . . .

. . . making a beautiful rainbow.

sunlight

raindrop

1

2

3

When Is the Best Time to Look for Rainbows?

It's best to go rainbow hunting right after it rains, and when the sun is shining low in the sky (a few hours after sunrise or a few hours before sunset).

Why that time?

If the sun is too high in the sky, then you can't see a rainbow. An easy way to tell if the sun is in the right spot is to look at your shadow. When your shadow is taller than you, it's rainbow hunting time!

You also need to place yourself in the right spot. After the clouds have cleared away from the sun, stand with the sun behind you.

TIP: If it's sunny out, try looking for rainbows in a waterfall!

HOSE RAINBOWS

When it's sunny outside, cool off your toes and make pretty rainbows with a hose.

1. Go outside! Turn on a hose.

2. Face away from the sun. Point the hose so the sunlight hits the water.

3. Look around. Do you see any rainbows?

HEY! You got me all wet!

There it is—a RAINBOW!

TIP: If you can't go outdoors, try looking for rainbows in a sink near a sunny window.

What's Happening?

When the sunshine hits the mist from your hose, the light **refracts** and splits into different colors as it passes through each water droplet. The different colors are then **reflected** back at you, so you see a rainbow! (See diagram on page 5.)

RAINDROP IN A BAG

Make a raindrop using a plastic baggie.
Then, go test out this rainbow fact:
A raindrop can make light refract.

1. Fill a **plastic baggie** with water, and seal or twist it closed.

2. Hold up a piece of **white paper** so the sun shines directly on it.

3. Hold your baggie in the sun's path, so the light travels through the water before hitting the paper.

4. Move the baggie closer and farther away from the paper slowly until you find a rainbow.

TIP: When you are done finding rainbows, you can use your water-filled baggie as a magnifying glass!

What's Happening?

Your water-filled plastic baggie acts like a raindrop. When the sunlight passes through the water it bends and breaks apart into the different colors (see the diagram on page 5).

CAPTURE A RAINBOW

Catch a rainbow, then make your mark.
Trace a colorful rainbow arc.

1. Fill a **clear glass** about halfway with **water**.

2. Place your glass near the edge of a table and place a piece of **white paper** on the floor.

3. Crumple up a **dish towel**, then use it to prop up a **flashlight**.

4. Shine the flashlight through the glass toward your paper. Try different angles until a rainbow appears on the paper.

5. Trace the rainbow onto the paper using **crayons**.

6. Experiment with different sizes of glasses or jars and different amounts of water. Which combinations make the best rainbows?

TIP: For extra fun, try using multiple flashlights. How many rainbows can you make?

What's Happening?

Your flashlight is like the sun, and the water in your glass is like a raindrop. When the light shines through your glass at an angle, it bends and produces a rainbow. In nature, not all rainbows look the same. Bigger raindrops create brighter-looking rainbows. Some rainbows may be narrow, and others wide. What different rainbows can you make?

How Many Colors Are in a Rainbow?

Most pictures you see of rainbows show just six or seven colors. These colors are **red**, orange, yellow, **green**, **blue**, **purple**, and sometimes **indigo** (a color in between blue and purple).

But in nature, there are more than seven colors. That's because there are lots of colors in between those seven, like lime green and light blue.

This is called a **spectrum**, which basically means there are too many colors to count!

FUN FACT
Jumping spiders and bees can see ultraviolet colors, which are invisible to us!

Light travels in waves, like the ripples in the ocean. Scientists measure light by finding the distance between the top of one wave and the top of the next wave. This is called the **wavelength**.

Each color has a different wavelength. The colors in a spectrum are arranged in a certain order, according to their wavelength. Purple light has the shortest wavelength. Red light has the longest wavelength.

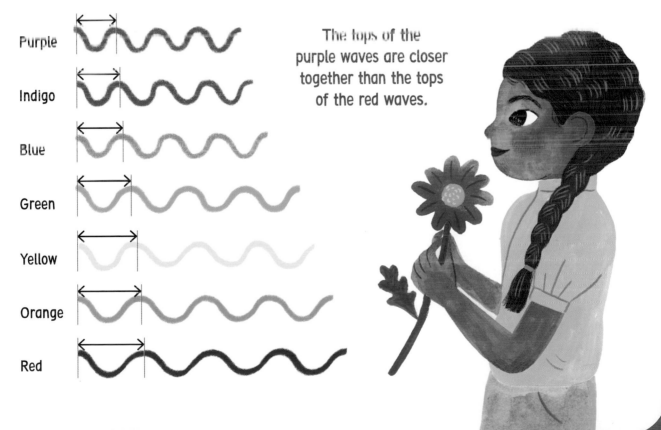

Purple

Indigo

Blue

Green

Yellow

Orange

Red

The tops of the purple waves are closer together than the tops of the red waves.

COLOR WHEEL SPINNER

See how all the colors of the rainbow become white when mixed together. For some dizzy rainbow fun, watch spinning colors blend to one.

1. Divide a **white paper plate** into six parts using a **ruler** and a **pencil**. (Draw a line down the middle, then draw two more lines to make six triangular "slices" like a pizza.)

2. Using **crayons** or **markers**, color each slice one of the colors of the rainbow.

3. Poke the pencil through the center of the plate (be careful not to poke yourself!) and **tape** the pencil to the plate so it looks like an umbrella.

4. Roll the pencil in between your hands quickly, making the plate spin. Or try pushing the pencil further through the hole in the plate and spin it on the floor like a top.

5. Watch the colors—what happens when your color wheel spins quickly?

What's Happening?

When you spin the color wheel, the colors mix, making them look white. White light, like sunlight, contains all the colors of the rainbow!

Why Do Things Appear to Be Different Colors?

When light waves hit an object, like a basketball, some of the color waves get absorbed into the object.

Other light waves **reflect** when they hit the object. **The light waves that reflect are the colors we see.**

Which colors get absorbed and which are reflected depend on the properties of the object.

What happens when you shine a colored light on an object?

Remember that white light contains all the colors. So, if you shine white light onto a red shirt, it appears red because the red light is reflected and all the other colors are absorbed into the shirt.

But if you shine a blue light onto a red shirt, the shirt would appear black. That's because there is no red light to reflect.

RIDDLE:
How does a rainbow say hello?

A. With a light wave.

COLOR QUEST

Get ready for a color quest. Which rainbow color do you like best?

1. Search around your house or outside for solid-colored objects in each of the colors of the rainbow: **red**, **orange**, **yellow**, **green**, **blue**, and **purple**.

2. Collect the things you find. Which colors are the easiest to find? Which ones are more difficult? In nature, the rarest color is blue.

3. Arrange your found objects into the shape of a rainbow!

EXTRA: Have a friend or family member go on a color quest, too. What objects did they find for each color? Were any of them the same as yours?

Hey, what are you doing?

I'm making
a rainbow!

21

CANDY COLORS

Where do you think the colors will go when you dissolve a candy rainbow?

1. Arrange **colored candies**, such as Skittles or M&Ms, in a circle around the edge of a **white plate**, placing the colors in the order of the rainbow.

2. Pour enough **warm water** into the center of the plate to fill the plate and reach the candies.

3. Watch what happens to the colors.

4. Try it again, but this time, group the candies together. How many different candy rainbows can you make? What happens if you shake the plate?

RIDDLE: Why are rainbows bad liars?

A. They always show their true colors.

What's Happening?

The sugar molecules in the colored candy coating are attracted to the water molecules, like a magnet attracting a metal paper clip. The dyed sugar moves through the water as it dissolves and mixes with the water.

23

How Do Eyes See Color?

The special cells in our eyes that help us see color are called **cones**. The cones are in the back of our eye, in a part called the retina.

Retina

Here's a close-up of the retina. See the cones?

There are three kinds of cones in our eyes. Each cone can see a range of colors but is best at seeing one color (blue, green, or red).

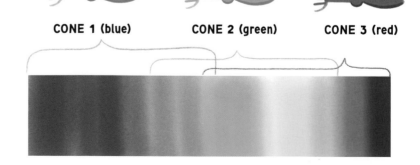

CONE 1 (blue)   CONE 2 (green)   CONE 3 (red)

Different cones in our eyes work together to see different colors.

For example, when the color yellow hits our eyes, the red cone and the green cone both react and signal to our brain that we see yellow.

This is how we can see many different shades of colors, even though we have only blue, green, and red cones in our eyes.

Some people have four types of cones, so they can see even more colors—up to 100 times more! Other people have only two types of cones, and they have a color vision deficiency.

Special glasses help people with a color vision deficiency see all the colors!

COLOR VISION TEST

All colors look different, but do you have a clue if the blue your friends see is the same blue as you?

1. Draw 20 small circles on a piece of **white paper** by tracing a **penny**.

2. Using your favorite color **crayon** or **marker**, color in a group of circles to make the first letter of your name.

3. Color the rest of the circles using a different color.

4. Look at your letter. Is it easy or hard to tell what it is?

EXTRA: You could even try writing a fun message or making a picture of an eye using colored dots!

5

→ 4

What's Happening?

People who have a color vision deficiency (color blindness) can usually still see colors, but they can't see the difference between certain colors, like red, green, and blue. A doctor might check a person's color vision using pictures of letters made with colored dots, like the one you made! If a person cannot see the letter in the middle of the grid, they might be color-blind.

RAINBOW VOLCANO

Mix up some colors and try not to panic. This chemistry experiment is truly volcanic!

1. Place six small **plastic cups** in a large **bowl** or a sink.

2. Add 1 teaspoon of **baking soda** to each cup.

3. Using a set of assorted food coloring, add 3 drops of red **food coloring** to cup one and 3 drops of orange food coloring to cup two. Continue, adding 3 drops of each of the other rainbow colors to the other four cups. Then use a **spoon** to mix it in.

4. Pour about 2 cups of **white vinegar** into the cups, dividing it evenly.

5. Stand back and watch your rainbow volcano explode!

EXTRA: Next time, try dyeing the vinegar, then see what happens when you add the colored vinegar to the colored baking soda. What colors can you make?

What's Happening?

When vinegar and baking soda mix together in your volcano, they make carbon dioxide. You may have heard of carbon dioxide before—it's the molecule that makes the bubbles in soda, and it's what makes the bubbles in your rainbow volcano!

In 2021 in Hawaii, a rainbow formed above Kilauea volcano as it was erupting!

Why Do We See Rainbows in Soap Bubbles?

Bubbles don't make rainbows in the same way that raindrops make rainbows. A bubble is made when soap combines with water and traps air. The wall of a bubble is made of three thin layers: soap, water in the middle, and another layer of soap.

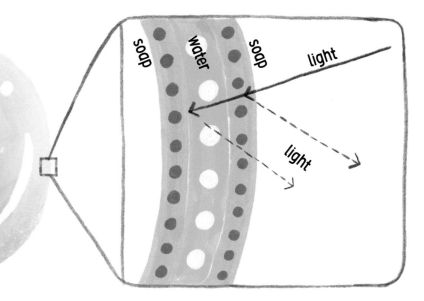

soap water soap

light

light

When light waves hit bubbles, some of the light reflects back at you from the outer soap layer, and some light reflects back from the inner soap layer.

The colors you see in a bubble change over time, so you may not see all the colors of the rainbow at the same time.

This is because gravity makes water slide down the inside of the bubble, making the bubble walls thinner. This changes how much light is reflected back at you, and what colors you see.

BUBBLE RAINBOWS

To make some cool rainbows, blow a big bubble. Do this outside to avoid bubble trouble.

1. Measure ¼ cup **water**, 1 tablespoon **dish detergent**, and 2 tablespoons **sugar** into a bowl.

2. Stir gently until the sugar dissolves. Now you have your bubble solution!

3. Dip a **spoon with holes** into your bubble solution, then lift it out. There should be bubble solution in the holes on the spoon.

4. Blow gently at the holes on the spoon to make bubbles.

5. Spot some rainbows in your bubbles.

SOAP

BUBBLE TIME!

EXTRA: Try bending a pipe cleaner into a square or a triangle—or a totally unique shape!—to make a bubble wand. Is the bubble you make a different shape? Or is it still round?

Light waves are reflected back to you from the outside and the inside of the bubbles. As the walls of the bubbles grow thinner, less light is reflected back at you and you see different colors.

I see a rainbow in my bubble!

RAINBOW REFLECTIONS

Water droplets aren't the only things that can make rainbows. Shine a light on a CD. How many rainbows can you see?

1. Hold your **CD** with the shiny side facing something white.

2. Shine your **flashlight** onto the shiny side of the CD.

3. Spot the rainbow!

What's Happening?

CDs are made by stamping bumps into plastic. When light waves reflect off these bumps, the waves interact with each other and produce a rainbow. Just like when light hits a bubble, some waves come together to make certain colors brighter, and other waves cancel each other out to take away certain colors.

RIDDLE: Why did the rainbow get seasick?

A. There were lots of waves.

RAINBOW PAPER

Have you seen rainbows in puddles on the street? Find out why this happens while you make something neat!

1. Pour **water** into a **small bowl**.

2. Add a drop of **clear nail polish** to the water.

3. Dip a piece of **black construction paper** into the water and pull it out quickly. (Tip: Hold the edge of the paper so you don't get nail polish on your fingers.)

4. Look at the rainbows on your paper!

What's Happening?

The thin layer, or film, of nail polish on your paper is thicker in some places than in others. This makes the light travel different distances and reflect back different colors. Try tipping your paper in different directions. How do your rainbows change? When oil drips from cars into puddles, it doesn't mix with the water. The oil floats on top of the water and reflects light just like the nail polish. So, watch out for rainbows on the road!

What Is a Double Rainbow?

Sometimes in nature you can see a double rainbow! This happens when light reflects twice in the same raindrop. The first reflection creates the main rainbow, and the second reflection creates the second rainbow.

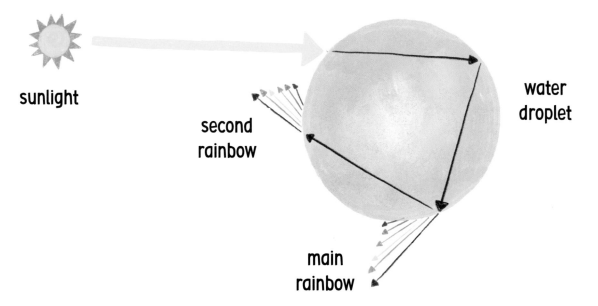

sunlight

second
rainbow

water
droplet

main
rainbow

The colors in the second rainbow appear in the opposite order, just the way things are reversed when you look in a mirror. The second rainbow is usually lighter than the main rainbow because all that light doesn't make it to our eyes.

The space between the two rainbows, called **Alexander's Band**, is darker than the rest of the sky. That's because the droplets there are refracting light that doesn't reach our eyes.

COLORFUL KALEIDOSCOPE

Kaleidoscopes make use of light, to reflect a pretty sight.

1. Gather tiny translucent (see-through) objects, such as **plastic beads**. Place your objects in a **plastic baggie**, then seal the baggie.

TIP: Check if an object is **translucent** by holding it up to a light. If you can see some light through it, then it is translucent! You can make some translucent objects by coloring bits of clear plastic (such as from disposable plastic containers) with a colored permanent marker.

2. Find an **empty chip bag** with a shiny inside and an **empty cereal box**. Cut them both into rectangles about the same size as a piece of printer paper. If your chip bag is small, just fold the paper in half and measure using that!

3. **Glue** the chip bag rectangle, shiny side out, onto the cereal box rectangle. Wait for it to dry.

Turn the page to continue the activity. ➔

4. Fold your rectangle in half like a book, shiny side in, and make a crease.

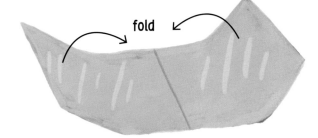

crease ⟶

5. Open it back up, then fold the two ends of the rectangle inwards, so they meet at the crease in the middle, like a set of double doors.

fold

6. Make two creases at the folds.

crease

crease ⟶

TIP: The kaleidoscope will work best if you keep the edges very crisp and the shiny surfaces as smooth as possible!

7. Then open the rectangle back up again.

8. Bend the rectangle along the crease lines into a three-sided box, with the shiny part on the inside. One side will have two layers.

9. Using a **rubber band**, attach the baggie onto the end of your triangle so it looks like a window with things stuck to it.

10. Point your kaleidoscope toward a light (don't look directly at the sun!). Look through the open end so you can see your objects reflect.

What's Happening?

Kaleidoscopes make colorful patterns using the same science that creates double rainbows! When light hits a shiny surface, like your chip bag, it is reflected. Since there are multiple shiny surfaces in your kaleidoscope, the light gets reflected multiple times, so you see your small objects multiple times.

How Do Rainbow Glasses Work?

The lenses of your rainbow glasses contain hundreds of little slits. Together these make what is called a diffraction grating.

As light passes through these slits, the light waves are broken apart into different colors, like when you squish a ball of dough through a grater or sieve, and it separates into pieces. This is called **diffraction**.

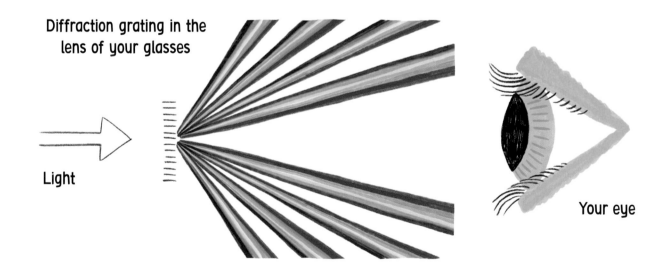

Diffraction grating in the lens of your glasses

Light

Your eye

To use your rainbow glasses, look at light. If you're outside, get in a sunny spot (but don't stare at the sun!).

If you're inside, look at a light bulb. Different types of light bulbs will make different-colored rainbows. Go around your home.

How many different types of rainbows can you see?

RAINBOW SCIENCE TERMS

Alexander's Band: The dark band between the two rainbows in a double rainbow

angle: The measurement of the corner where two lines meet.

cones: The cells in your eyes that let you see color

diffraction: When light hits something and is broken up into different colors as it bends around it

double rainbow: When light is refracted twice by each raindrop, and you can see two rainbows in which the colors appear in opposite order

lab journal: A notebook used to write down observations and scientific discoveries

light wave: The path light takes as it travels through space

reflect: When light bounces off of something

refract: When light changes direction while traveling through something

spectroscopy: The science of how light interacts with objects and breaks into rainbows

spectrum: The range of all the colors in the rainbow

translucent object: An object that light can pass through

wavelength: The distance between one high point and the next in a light wave

RAINBOW WONDER

When scientists do experiments, they write down everything they do in a **lab journal**. Use these questions to start your own rainbow journal!

Where are some places you have seen rainbows?

What questions do you have about rainbows?

How did you change the experiments to make them better?

Which experiment was easy?

What new experiments can you design?

Which experiment was the hardest?

The mission of Storey Publishing is to serve our customers by publishing practical information that encourages personal independence in harmony with the environment.

Edited by Deanna F. Cook and Sarah Guare Slattery
Art direction and book design by Jessica Armstrong
Text production by Jennifer Jepson Smith
Illustrations by © Sarah Walsh/Lilla Rogers Studio

Storey books are available at special discounts when purchased in bulk for premiums and sales promotions as well as for fund-raising or educational use. Special editions or book excerpts can also be created to specification. For details, please send an email to special.markets@hbgusa.com.

Storey Publishing
210 MASS MoCA Way
North Adams, MA 01247
storey.com

Storey Publishing is an imprint of Workman Publishing, a division of Hachette Book Group, Inc., 1290 Avenue of the Americas, New York, NY 10104.

Distributed in Europe by Hachette Livre, 58 rue Jean Bleuzen, 92 178 Vanves Cedex, France
Distributed in the United Kingdom by Hachette Book Group, UK, Carmelite House, 50 Victoria Embankment, London EC4Y 0DZ

ISBNs: 978-1-63586-617-9 (Paper over board with prism glasses); 978-1-63586-618-6 (Fixed Format EPUB eBook); 978-1-63586-835-7 (Fixed Format PDF); 978-1-63586-836-4 (Fixed Format Kindle eBook)

Printed in China by R. R. Donnelley on paper from responsible sources
10 9 8 7 6 5 4 3 2 1

Library of Congress Cataloging-in-Publication Data on file